YORK NOTES

I'm the King of the Castle

Susan Hill

Notes by Caroline Woolfe

 Longman   York Press

YORK PRESS
322 Old Brompton Road, London SW5 9JH

Pearson Education Limited
Edinburgh Gate, Harlow,
Essex CM20 2JE, United Kingdom
Associated companies, branches and representatives throughout the world

First published 1997
18

ISBN: 978-0-582-31381-1

Designed by Vicki Pacey, Trojan Horse
Illustrated by Susan Scott
Map by Valerie Hill
Typeset by Pantek Arts, Maidstone, Kent
Phototypeset by Gem Graphics, Trenance, Mawgan Porth, Cornwall
Colour reproduction and film output by Spectrum Colour
Printed in China
(CTPS/18)

CONTENTS

PREFACE

York Notes are designed to give you a broader perspective on works of literature studied at GCSE and equivalent levels. We have carried out extensive research into the needs of the modern literature student prior to publishing this new edition. Our research showed that no existing series fully met students' requirements. Rather than present a single authoritative approach, we have provided alternative viewpoints, empowering students to reach their own interpretations of the text. York Notes provide a close examination of the work and include biographical and historical background, summaries, glossaries, analyses of characters, themes, structure and language, cultural connections and literary terms.

If you look at the Contents page you will see the structure for the series. However, there's no need to read from the beginning to the end as you would with a novel, play, poem or short story. Use the Notes in the way that suits you. Our aim is to help you with your understanding of the work, not to dictate how you should learn.

York Notes are written by English teachers and examiners, with an expert knowledge of the subject. They show you how to succeed in coursework and examination assignments, guiding you through the text and offering practical advice. Questions and comments will extend, test and reinforce your knowledge. Attractive colour design and illustrations improve clarity and understanding, making these Notes easy to use and handy for quick reference.

York Notes are ideal for:
- Essay writing
- Exam preparation
- Class discussion

The author of these Notes is Caroline Woolfe who studied English Literature at Manchester University. She is an experienced teacher of English in schools and colleges, where she has prepared students for public examinations at all levels. She is a senior GCSE examiner.

The text used in these Notes is the Longman Imprint Books edition, 1981.

Health Warning: **This study guide will enhance your understanding, but should not replace the reading of the original text and/or study in class.**

Part one

Introduction

How to study a novel

You have bought this book because you wanted to study a novel on your own. This may supplement classwork.

- You will need to read the novel several times. Start by reading it quickly for pleasure, then read it slowly and carefully. Further readings will generate new ideas and help you to memorise the details of the story.
- Make careful notes on themes, plot and characters of the novel. The plot will change some of the characters. Who changes?
- The novel may not present events chronologically. Does the novel you are reading begin at the beginning of the story or does it contain flashbacks and a muddled time sequence? Can you think why?
- How is the story told? Is it narrated by one of the characters or by an all-seeing ('omniscient') narrator?
- Does the same person tell the story all the way through? Or do we see the events through the minds and feelings of a number of different people?
- Which characters does the narrator like? Which characters do you like or dislike? Do your sympathies change during the course of the book? Why? When?
- Any piece of writing (including your notes and essays) is the result of thousands of choices. No book had to be written in just one way: the author could have chosen other words, other phrases, other characters, other events. How could the author of your novel have written the story differently? If events were recounted by a minor character how would this change the novel?

Studying on your own requires self-discipline and a carefully thought-out work plan in order to be effective. Good luck.

SUSAN HILL'S BACKGROUND

Biographical
details

Susan Hill was born in 1942. She grew up happily as an only child in Scarborough, Yorkshire, a town which she remembers with affection. At the age of 16 she moved with her parents to Coventry in the Midlands.

From a young age she developed a love of reading which led her from grammar school to study literature at King's College, London.

She has lived in Leamington Spa and Stratford, places deliberately chosen for their charm and atmosphere. During her most prolific period of creative writing, she would escape to the peacefulness of the Dorset countryside, or to a small seaside town in Suffolk, for inspiration for her novels. It was whilst staying in a remote cottage in Dorset that she wrote *I'm the King of the Castle*. In this novel, as in all her work, her evocative descriptions reflect her familiarity with the natural landscape and her deep affection for the English countryside.

You should consider
the influence of
places in this novel
and the importance
of the setting chosen
by the author.

In 1975, she met and married Stanley Wells, a Shakespeare scholar. Following the birth of their first child, the family moved from Stratford into the Oxfordshire countryside. They now have two daughters and live in Gloucestershire.

Susan Hill has a strong sense of place. She has written autobiographically about the places in which she has lived, exploring her belief that places are influential in making people what they are.

Other works

Susan Hill is a popular and distinguished writer. Looking back, she is unable to identify exactly when she became a writer, having always had an inner life of creativity and imagination. Perhaps it is unsurprising then that her first book was published when she was only nineteen years old, and she has gone on to produce many acclaimed works. During a period of remarkable creativity between 1968 and 1974, she wrote six novels, two collections of short stories and several radio plays.

I'm the King of the Castle, *The Albatross and Other Stories* and *The Bird of Night* have all won literary awards. *The Woman in Black* is a compelling ghost story which has also been staged as a play. Her books for children include *Can It Be True?* which won the Smarties prize. She has written two autobiographical books, *The Magic Apple Tree* and *Family*.

Her enthusiasm for literature is apparent in all her work. She is respected as a literary reviewer and broadcaster and has edited two books of short stories.

CONTEXT & SETTING

Susan Hill wrote this novel during the summer of 1969. Some references suggest a contemporary setting – the boys' jeans and anoraks, and Kingshaw's boast about his father's distant experience as a pilot in the war – but the timeless quality of its themes, and the isolated setting make the exact period irrelevant. This is a story of misery in childhood, which could happen at any time, but it is not a pessimistic view of children's experience in general. The events are linked closely to the particular circumstances of these families in this house. Fielding's presence is an important reminder that a more normal, happier world exists beyond them.

Many novels have been written about children. During the nineteenth century, writers explored the journey of the child into adulthood. Charlotte Brontë in *Jane Eyre*, and Charles Dickens in several of his novels, showed how childhood experience shaped and influenced characters in later life. Another function of children in literature has been to examine the adult world through their eyes. Mark Twain's *Huckleberry Finn* and *What*

Dreams are considered to be psychologically important. What do Kingshaw's dreams contribute to the novel?

Maisie Knew by Henry James gave a frank account of the adult world seen from the fresh perspective of children.

During the twentieth century, novelists have written in more detail about the psychology of their characters. They have explored the importance of past experiences and social relationships, and provided more insight into their characters' thoughts and feelings. By treating Kingshaw's feelings seriously, and showing the tragic result of his unhappiness, Susan Hill invites the reader to reconsider perceptions of childhood, and acknowledge the real existence of such misery.

SETTING

The social setting of the novel is amongst the English upper classes; the boys attend fee-paying boarding schools and call each other by their surnames. In this world of privilege and distinction, it is no wonder that Kingshaw is embarrassed by his family's present poverty, or that Hooper sees in it an opportunity to taunt him. It is a world in which boys must quickly learn to be independent of their parents, when they are sent away to school from the age of seven.

Warings

You should notice how Susan Hill creates an impression of the atmosphere of Warings as the setting for the novel.

Warings is a large house built by the first Joseph Hooper who was a successful businessman. Although the present Mr Hooper made no contribution to it, and knows himself to be unsuccessful and weak, he believes that the house will now provide him with the status which he claims as a right. Warings represents the Hooper family pride. Its collection of moths suggests their preoccupation with dead and useless things at the expense of family relationships. Hooper's close identification with the house makes it all the more hostile to Kingshaw, and its gloomy atmosphere makes him afraid.

y

Hang Wood and the wider setting

How does Susan Hill's description create a vivid impression of Hang Wood and the surrounding countryside?

In her introduction, Susan Hill says that she found her setting for this novel in the rural isolation of the West Country. Her imagination was stirred and her senses sharpened by its atmosphere. This setting is vividly evoked in her description, and firmly linked to Kingshaw's feelings. The countryside is sometimes shown as hostile to Kingshaw, perhaps to reflect his fearfulness and isolation. Hang Wood is like another world to him; at first he cannot find a way in, then is deeply affected by its atmosphere. In Hang Wood, Kingshaw appears to come alive. The description in this section suggests that his senses are more alert and he behaves more confidently. Most importantly, he discovers the stream – a haven of tranquillity and escape. The paradoxical (see Literary Terms) description of the wood as 'Terrifying and safe' (p. 119) conveys an image of the untamed natural environment. Its power and cruelty, shown through images like the storm and the sparrowhawk, are terrifying, but Kingshaw likes the remote feeling of the wood and the contentment of lying in the stream. At the end of the novel he is forced back to the wood by his great fear of what the future holds for him at school and at Warings.

PART TWO

SUMMARIES

GENERAL SUMMARY

Chapters 1–4: Warings – the struggle for control

The events occur during the summer holidays, at Warings, which is a gloomy house inherited by Edmund's father. Since his wife's death, Mr Hooper has had difficulty managing his son. He appoints a widow, Mrs Kingshaw, as 'informal housekeeper', intending that her son, Charles, will be company for Edmund.

The boys do not get on well. Hooper despises Kingshaw, who is a fearful and sensitive boy. Quickly realising that Kingshaw has many fears, Hooper bullies him. Kingshaw does not have the confidence to stop him.

Kingshaw decides to run away from Warings.

Chapters 5–9: Hang Wood

Hooper has thwarted Kingshaw's attempt to escape by following him to Hang Wood. In this unfamiliar environment, their different fears are explored, and the sense of power constantly shifts between them.

A tranquil clearing, where there is a stream, becomes a special place to Kingshaw and an important symbol of escape. Kingshaw tries to convince himself that the episode in the wood has changed things between himself and Hooper. He feels more able to cope with their return to Warings.

Chapters 10–13: The return to Warings

At Warings, Kingshaw's hope of an improvement in their relationship is disappointed. Hooper's bullying intensifies.

Kingshaw feels increasingly isolated. Preoccupied with her relationship with Mr Hooper, his mother refuses to believe what he tells her about Edmund. She accepts Mr Hooper's offer to pay for Charles to join Edmund at his boarding school.

An outing to a castle provides Kingshaw with a brief sense of power and escape. He climbs high up the ruined walls and shouts, 'I'm the king of the castle'. Hooper falls from a ledge and Kingshaw is suspected of pushing him.

Chapters 14–17: Suicide – the only answer

With Hooper in hospital, Kingshaw enjoys some respite from his persecution and makes a new friend. Fielding is an uncomplicated and happy boy, and appears to be exactly the friend that Kingshaw needs. However, Kingshaw's happiness in this new friendship is short-lived: Hooper returns from hospital and reasserts his power. Kingshaw begins to lose hope.

The adults, who have grown increasingly close, announce that their wedding will be held in the morning of the day on which the boys return to school together. Kingshaw's hopelessness intensifies when his friendship with Fielding is destroyed by his mother's insensitivity and Hooper's malice. In a gesture of revenge, he destroys some important things from Hooper's room, then immediately fears the consequences.

Kingshaw receives a threatening note from Hooper and all his fears overwhelm him. He knows that there is only one means of escape left to him. At dawn, he finds his way back to the stream in Hang Wood, and drowns himself.

Evil has triumphed, and Hooper is proud that his power forced Kingshaw to suicide.

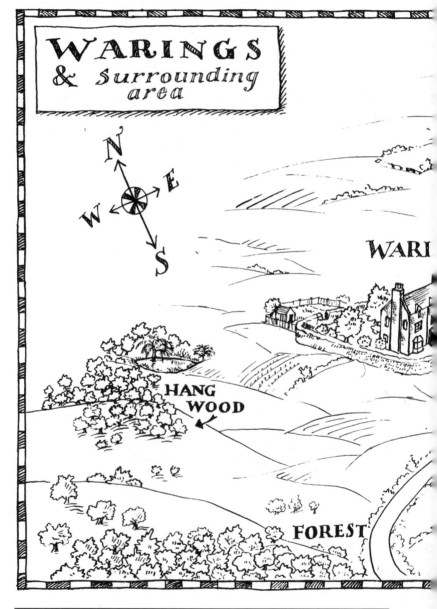

WARINGS
& Surrounding area

N
E
W
S

WARI

HANG WOOD

FOREST

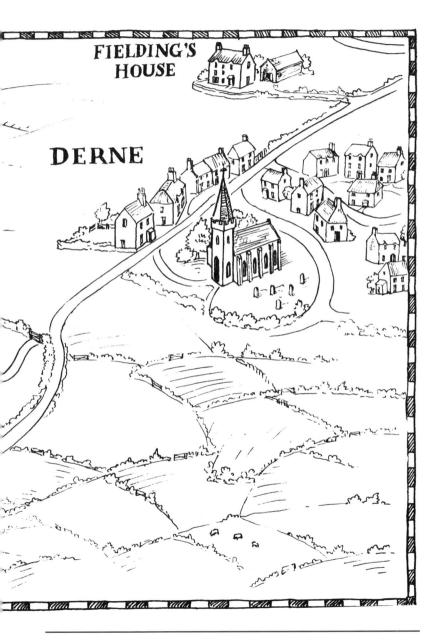

FIELDING'S HOUSE

DERNE

CHAPTER 1 The opening chapter introduces Mr Joseph Hooper and his ten-year-old son, Edmund. They have come to live at Warings, the Hooper family home, which Mr Hooper has inherited on the death of his father.

Mr Hooper had been estranged from his father by the lack of affection or understanding between them. Now there are similar difficulties in his relationship with Edmund.

Note the isolation of Warings shown on page 3. We are given a brief history of the Hooper family. The house, its grounds and the surrounding landscape are described in detail.

The Red Room is introduced. It is a room kept locked because it contains the valuable collection of moths and butterflies which belonged to Mr Hooper's father. Mr Hooper is reluctant to let Edmund into the room, but Edmund notes where his father keeps the key.

In the middle of the night, Edmund goes downstairs, takes the key from his father's desk and goes into the room. He explores the room, examining the museum-like collection of moths and butterflies in display cases. Fascinated by the specimens, he opens a glass case to look more closely at the Death's Head Hawk Moth. As he tries to pick it up, the whole moth disintegrates into dust.

Acheroptia Atropos

COMMENT   The house and its setting are key features in the novel. The description of Warings as an ugly house, holding no memories of family happiness, creates a sombre atmosphere from the beginning. The surrounding landscape, with its ancient yew trees and dark green rhododendrons reinforces the sense of gloom. We are shown the enduring nature of the surrounding landscape and its powerful presence in the mood it creates, and in the effects it has on the characters.

The flashback technique is used to explore Mr Hooper's bitter memories of his childhood – the misunderstanding and lack of communication between himself and his father (see Structure).

We begin to understand Edmund Hooper's character. In his father's eyes he is hard and inscrutable. We see his coolness towards others, his lack of fear in the house, his independence and his ability to defy his father.

The chapter begins and ends with images (see Literary Terms) of death. Consider how this contributes to the atmosphere of the opening chapter.

The disintegration of the moth might symbolise Hooper's takeover of the house, echoing the description of the 'moth-like whiteness' (p. 2) of his dying grandfather's skin.

GLOSSARY   **dynastic sense** a sense of the importance of being part of a family line, as kings are

yew trees evergreen trees which can live for hundreds of years. They are often found in English churchyards, and usually symbolise sadness because their branches were traditionally used as funeral decorations

WARINGS – THE STRUGGLE FOR CONTROL

CHAPTER 2

Mr Hooper has appointed an 'informal housekeeper' for a trial period over the summer holidays. Mrs Helena Kingshaw is a widow. Her ten-year-old son, Charles, will be a companion for Edmund.

When the Kingshaws arrive, Edmund stays in his room, watching secretly. He drops a note from his window to Charles Kingshaw telling him he doesn't want him at Warings.

Note the realistic speech and behaviour of the young boys.

During the boys' first encounter in Kingshaw's bedroom, Hooper aggressively questions Kingshaw about his background. He is contemptuous of Kingshaw's dead father and the Kingshaws' poverty. He boasts about his own position at Warings. Kingshaw tries to assert his authority in his own room, but fails, and the boys have a brief fight.

Mr Hooper reproaches his son for his unwelcoming behaviour, but is met only by insolence. Later, Edmund mockingly follows his father's instructions by forcing Kingshaw to accompany him on a tour of the house. He runs around every room, banging doors and showing off, until Kingshaw stops following him and sits quietly on the stairs. When Hooper walks menacingly down behind him, Kingshaw resists an urge to push him down the stairs. When Hooper has gone, he continues to sit there for a long time.

COMMENT

We learn more about the relationships between parents and children. Hooper spurns intimacy with his father (p. 10), who is frustrated by his failure to build a better relationship (p. 17). We are also given hints of the gulf that exists between Kingshaw and his mother when he blames her for the fight (p. 14), and feels ashamed of the way she had spoken of Warings (p. 15).

In the boys' first conversation we are shown Hooper's dominance. Kingshaw is disturbed by Hooper's hostility, but miserably acknowledges to himself that he is unable to do anything about it. There are opportunities in the novel, as on the stairs (p. 19), for Kingshaw to get his own back. Why doesn't he do so?

The themes of isolation and loneliness are important in the novel (see Themes). Different aspects of these themes are subtly introduced in relation to each of the characters:

- Edmund wants to be alone at Warings. He is angry and resentful of the intrusion of the Kingshaws
- Mr Hooper is 'alarmed' at the prospect of sharing his life with others (p. 10)
- Mrs Kingshaw 'had been much alone' before coming to Warings (p. 10)
- Charles Kingshaw would like to escape on his own from the torment of Edmund Hooper (p. 19)

GLOSSARY   cheval mirror a full-length mirror in a supporting frame

Battle of Britain a period during the Second World War when the German Luftwaffe's attempt to destroy the Royal Air Force and bomb its airfields was defeated

CHAPTER 3   To escape from Warings, Kingshaw walks into the surrounding countryside. Avoiding the gloomy copse, he walks over the fields. In a cornfield he is attacked by a swooping crow. He runs away, terrified, but the crow chases him. Kingshaw trips over and the crow lands on his back. After a few moments, frightened by his screams, it flies away.

Hooper watches the whole incident from an upstairs window of Warings. When Kingshaw returns, Hooper taunts him about his fear of the crow, and his reluctance to go into the copse. He dares Kingshaw to go into the copse, and into the larger Hang Wood. Kingshaw is resigned to accepting the dare.

Relishing his sense of power over Kingshaw, Hooper plans further torment. He puts a stuffed crow on Kingshaw's bed in the middle of the night, then waits outside the door for Kingshaw's reaction. Seeing the crow when he wakes, Kingshaw is 'faint with fear', but he steels himself to lie silently, reluctant to give Hooper the satisfaction of knowing how frightened he is. In the morning, when Kingshaw is in the lavatory, Hooper removes the crow.

The boys make no reference to the incident at breakfast, and their parents think they are getting on well.

Later, Hooper finds Kingshaw looking through the window of the Red Room. He offers to show him the 'valuable things' in there after supper. Kingshaw does not want to go into the room, but cannot admit this to Hooper. Entering the room, Kingshaw is repelled by the smell and the specimens in the cabinets. Hooper urges him further into the room, then runs out and locks Kingshaw in. Again, Kingshaw refuses to cry out and sits in torture, afraid of the moths, until he can casually call to Mr Hooper and Mrs Kingshaw as they pass the door. Avoiding their questions, he runs upstairs where he is violently sick in the lavatory.

Why does Susan Hill mention Kingshaw's happiness at school at the end of this chapter?

At the end of the chapter Kingshaw's thoughts return to his first day at St Vincent's school, the one place with which he feels familiar, and where he is secure and at ease.

COMMENT

There are images (see Literary Terms) of hostility in the description of Kingshaw's walk in the surrounding countryside (pp. 20–1):

- He stumbles over ruts, and the vegetation pricks his feet
- The sun burns his face and he is uncomfortably hot
- The crow characterises this hostility through its real physical attack on Kingshaw

The accumulation of these images conveys a sense of Kingshaw's isolation in this menacing environment.

In this chapter Hooper's approach to his torment of Kingshaw becomes systematic, 'having Kingshaw here, thinking of things to do to him' (p. 25). Although this situation is new to him, he quickly adapts to the role of persecutor, creating a disturbing sense of danger.

The security that Kingshaw feels at school is what he lacks in his family life. 'There, he belonged, they knew him, he had become the person they had all decided that he would be' (p. 33).

GLOSSARY   **stone-walling** stubborn resistance

CHAPTER 4   Kingshaw secretly adopts a small room at the top of the house as his own retreat from Hooper. Its appeal lies in its lack of character or obvious use, which gives him the confidence to take it over. He thinks about his hatred for Hooper, terrified by the strength of his feelings. Acknowledging that the relationship with Hooper at Warings will not change, he decides to run away.

What is implied when Hooper raises his eyebrow after Mr Hooper reminds him that Kingshaw has no father?

On a train journey to London with his father, Hooper reflects on the power he has gained over Kingshaw and considers how to discover his hiding place.

Kingshaw methodically collects things to take with him, and stores them in his secret room.

Their parents remain unaware of the hostility between the boys. Watching them play with a bagatelle game which Mr Hooper brings out for them, Mrs Kingshaw is delighted at their growing friendship.

When Hooper discovers Kingshaw's secret room, Kingshaw hopelessly lets him in. Seeing the things that Kingshaw has collected for his escape, Hooper guesses his intention. He is triumphant that his actions have forced

Kingshaw to run away and, delighting in his power, declares that he will go with him. Kingshaw is dismayed, but resigned that Hooper will carry out his threat.

Still blind to the true relationship between the boys, Mr Hooper reflects on the success of his new domestic arrangements. He and Mrs Kingshaw are 'gratified with one another', and they plan to hold a cocktail party to mark the beginning of their new lives.

COMMENT

What does Kingshaw mean when he considers himself to be 'proud' in contrast to his mother?

The description of Kingshaw's secret room (p. 35) relates to his character. He considers that this room is right for him because it 'had no character of its own'. This shows his realisation that he does not have the strength of character to overcome someone else's influence, and gives another reason why he is so ill-at-ease at Warings.

The juxtaposition of the boys' thoughts at the beginning of the chapter emphasises how their actions are inextricably linked. This interlude, when Hooper is away from Warings, allows each to assess the relationship and make plans.

As the hostility between the boys intensifies, their parents become more remote and two-dimensional (see Literary Terms). Mrs Kingshaw is determinedly cheerful. Several references are made to the bracelets which slide up and down her arm, perhaps representing her superficiality and flirtatiousness. Their decision to hold a cocktail party, traditionally seen as an artificial social occasion, suggests that they are concerned only with shallow relationships.

Even at this early stage, Kingshaw senses the potential danger of a battle with Hooper, and the difficulty of avoiding it at Warings.

A *Identify the characters 'to whom' these quotations refer.*

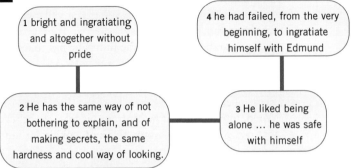

1 bright and ingratiating and altogether without pride

4 he had failed, from the very beginning, to ingratiate himself with Edmund

2 He has the same way of not bothering to explain, and of making secrets, the same hardness and cool way of looking.

3 He liked being alone … he was safe with himself

Identify the places described as follows.

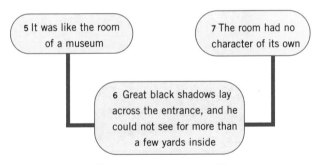

5 It was like the room of a museum

7 The room had no character of its own

6 Great black shadows lay across the entrance, and he could not see for more than a few yards inside

Check your answers on page 78.

B *Consider these issues.*

a How the atmosphere of Warings affects Kingshaw.

b The author's purpose in using flashback to the earlier lives of some of the characters.

c The realism of the speech and behaviour of Hooper and Kingshaw.

d The nature of the relationships in the Hooper and Kingshaw families.

e How the loneliness of each character is shown through their thoughts.

f How Kingshaw's fatalistic acceptance of Hooper is shown, and the impression it gives of his character.

HANG WOOD

CHAPTER 5   Kingshaw's mother tells him that she and Mr Hooper
are going to London on the following day to do the
shopping for the cocktail party. He decides to take this
opportunity to run away, knowing that it will give him a
full day before his absence is discovered. He makes the
final preparations, packing the things he has collected
into an old satchel.

At dawn the next day he sets off through a damp mist.
Remembering Hooper's dare, he makes for Hang
Wood, forcing himself to confront his fear. He believes
that not even Hooper would think of looking for him
there.

Arriving at the wood, he realises that it will be difficult
to enter. There is an overgrown ditch, a thick hedge and
a barbed wire fence. He follows the edge of the wood,
looking for a way in. As the mist clears, he feels more
confident and begins to congratulate himself on his
resourcefulness. He believes that his escape marks a
new period of greater self-confidence. He is brought up
short, however, and his self-doubt returns when he
discovers a wart on the back of his hand. He remembers
a superstitious story from school that one can get rid of
warts by wishing them on to someone else. He believes

that this wart has been wished on to him by an unfriendly boy called Broughton-Smith. It makes him feel afraid.

A little later, when the sun is fully up, he finds a gap in the hedge. He jumps over the ditch and steps quickly with his eyes closed into Hang Wood.

COMMENT   Susan Hill's description of Kingshaw's walk appeals vividly to the reader's senses. The simple language and detailed description conveys an image of the beauty of this deserted scene. Read pages 51–52 carefully to see how this is achieved.

There are signs that Mr Hooper and Mrs Kingshaw are becoming fond of each other: she is excited to be going to London; he invites her into his own sitting room.

Hooper is almost entirely absent from this chapter, showing perhaps that Kingshaw has taken the initiative. Suspense is created: does Hooper know that Kingshaw has gone?

CHAPTER 6   We are given a description of the dense wood. Kingshaw is surprised to find that he likes being hidden in there. He likes the smell of the wood and its sense of innocence.

The mood changes when Kingshaw hears the sound of something approaching. It is Hooper. Kingshaw realises that it was inevitable that Hooper would find him. He tries to persuade Hooper not to accompany him, but Hooper assumes his usual dominant role, taunting Kingshaw about his mother's position in the house.

Kingshaw's pleasure in the wood has gone. He starts to walk, pushing through the dense undergrowth with Hooper following him.

HANG WOOD

Kingshaw is 'somehow reassured by Hooper's close presence, by the ordinary smell of him'.

They hear the sound of an animal and see that it is a deer in a clearing in front of them. As Kingshaw hesitates, Hooper suggests that they stalk it, and he takes the lead.

For some time, Kingshaw follows him, but he feels angry that Hooper is once again in control. He tells Hooper that he wants to leave the wood now and carry on to where he was going. Arguing about the way to the edge of the wood, they realise that they are lost. Hooper collapses in fear and the chapter ends with the sound of an approaching storm.

COMMENT

Our impression of the innocence of the wood is enhanced by the description of the birdsong, the gentle 'cooing' of the pigeons and the presence of the artless rabbit. Notice how the change of mood is conveyed when Hooper approaches. The images (see Literary Terms) are harsher: the holly bush smells 'bitter' and a bird makes the sound of a 'mad person laughing'.

Hooper's presence not only frightens Kingshaw, it also has a disturbing effect on his mind. He loses control of his reason and behaves almost involuntarily. The description of Kingshaw's thoughts (p. 61), gives a frightening insight into his mental torment.

Kingshaw believes that, in the wood, he and Hooper are equal. You should be aware of the shifting balance of power between them as you read this section.

GLOSSARY   **get his bearings** to establish a sense of direction

CHAPTER 7

Kingshaw is surprised to find that the threat of a thunderstorm makes Hooper sick with fear. In a reversal of roles, Kingshaw calmly makes a shelter by throwing his anorak over the top of some thick bushes, whilst Hooper watches him, reduced by terror to babyish whimpering.

Kingshaw is uncertain how to deal with Hooper. Instead of the vindictiveness which the reader might feel he deserves, Kingshaw shows him an embarrassed sympathy. Hooper is so overcome with fear that he is unaware of Kingshaw's words.

How does Susan Hill's description of the storm make it vivid to the reader?

The violent storm ends abruptly. Hearing the sound of a stream, Kingshaw suggests going to it for a drink. He thinks that the events during the storm will have changed things between them, but Hooper apparently forgets his fearful behaviour, and again asserts his leadership. Kingshaw can only follow him dumbly.

Kingshaw finds a dead rabbit and picks it up curiously. Hooper urges him to throw it away, dismissing dead things as unimportant and boasting about having seen his dead grandfather. Kingshaw tries to express his view that humans are different, but Hooper mocks his belief, taunting him with the notion of ghosts. Kingshaw feels confused after the argument. Looking more closely at the rabbit, he notices a rotting wound inside its ear. He throws the rabbit away from him in disgust and fear. Hooper realises how Kingshaw feels, and is pleased to have made him afraid.

Note how the stream affects the boys.

They find the stream and Hooper insists that they follow it in the hope that it will lead them out of the wood. After some time, the stream runs into a clearing where it forms a pool. Hooper immediately decides to swim. At first, Kingshaw is reluctant to join him, remembering his fear of the swimming pool when he was younger. He decides that this pool is different, and jumps in. He finds the experience exhilarating, and for a time his hatred of Hooper is forgotten.

Hungry and cold after the swim, Kingshaw suggests lighting a fire. He feels a sense of responsibility and is impatient with Hooper for treating everything as a game. He begins to feel more able to cope with

Hooper, but Hooper refuses to relinquish his hold over Kingshaw. By reminding him of the moths which will come out at night, he rekindles Kingshaw's fear.

The balance of power continues to shift between them. When Hooper realises they are lost in the wood, he reacts hysterically. Kingshaw congratulates himself on his own presence of mind. He decides to try to find a way out, using the ball of string to prevent him getting lost. He leaves Hooper trying to catch a fish.

Walking through the wood alone, he is excited by this new world. He would like to go off alone, but, in spite of his hatred and fear, he feels responsible for Hooper.

He returns to the clearing. At first he cannot see Hooper, then finds him face down in the water. He drags Hooper away from the water and manages to revive him. He lights the fire and does his best to make Hooper comfortable. We see the range of his emotions, from fear that Hooper has died to elation at his own ability to cope with the crisis.

At the end of the chapter, he tells Hooper that they are still lost.

COMMENT   In this chapter the struggle for power is closely linked to the experience of fear. Hooper and Kingshaw each feel a sense of control when the other is frightened.

Kingshaw is shown to have a conscience: he cannot leave Hooper alone in the wood. Hooper, however, seems to be untroubled by any moral scruple. You should consider the importance of this in your assessment of their characters.

The novel explores the nature of fear. Kingshaw reflects on the difference between his own terror at 'dreaming his own fear' and Hooper's fear, which 'was a straightforward response to an outside situation'. Which type of fear do you consider the most powerful?

The stream is introduced and becomes an important symbol (see Literary Terms) in the novel. Consider the traditional symbolic associations of water, and the significance of this place to Kingshaw and Hooper.

The description of the storm is vivid. Again, the author uses simple images (see Literary Terms) to appeal to our senses. The presence of Hooper, terrified, emphasises the power of the storm as does the contrast in the scene when it ends.

GLOSSARY   **'Somebody did that once in history and they got away from a bull'** in Greek mythology, Theseus went to Crete to kill the minotaur, a monster which was half man, half bull. Ariadne, daughter of Minos, king of Crete, gave Theseus a ball of string to unravel on his way into the labyrinth where the monster was kept. After killing the minotaur, Theseus used the string to find his way out

CHAPTER 8   As it goes dark, the boys sit close to the fire. Kingshaw catches a fish. Unable to kill or gut it, he leaves it to die, then skewers it to be cooked unsuccessfully on the fire. Hooper maintains a steady criticism of Kingshaw's efforts, although he shows no practical skills of his own.

Wondering if their absence has been discovered, Hooper talks about their parents. He mocks Kingshaw's mother's habit of kissing him goodnight, then claims that she came to Warings only in search of a husband. Kingshaw is stunned by Hooper's revelation that their parents are likely to marry. Now that it has been pointed out to him, he can see the truth of it by reflecting on his mother's behaviour. He hates her, but feels guilty and worried in a superstitious way about the strength of his feelings.

As Hooper sleeps, Kingshaw thinks about recent events. Here in the wood he feels unafraid and distanced from all that troubled him at Warings. When the fire dies down feelings of fear and isolation overtake him. Eventually, he falls asleep.

Kingshaw wakes first and hears Hooper crying out in his sleep. He seems hysterical, and calls repeatedly for his mother. Kingshaw slaps his face to wake him.

Irritated by Hooper's presence, Kingshaw is drawn to the tranquillity of the pool.

What prevents Kingshaw from taking advantage of Hooper?

Hooper becomes increasingly afraid of not being found, and suspicious that Kingshaw will leave him. Like a demanding child, he nags Kingshaw to promise not to leave him. Incensed by his persistence, Kingshaw loses his temper. He shouts at Hooper and threatens to beat him. Hooper cowers in fear. Kingshaw, shocked at his own violent feelings, walks away.

When they return to the fire, Hooper refuses to speak to him. Kingshaw's conscience makes him reassure Hooper. Although he acknowledges to himself that this will lose him any advantage he might have gained, he feels that it is unimportant: he is stronger and more resourceful, and things have changed between them.

COMMENT

More differences in the characters of the boys are shown in this chapter: Kingshaw has the resourcefulness and practical skills to survive, whilst Hooper can only criticise. On the other hand, Hooper shows his awareness of more worldly affairs when he reveals to Kingshaw the relationship between their parents. Kingshaw's scruples are shown: he is unable to kill and gut the fish, and stops himself attacking Hooper. Hooper, who seems always to be in control, is seen as fearful and dependent.

Do you share Kingshaw's confidence that events in the wood have changed something in their relationship?

Consider why Kingshaw is drawn to the stream.

Kingshaw's feelings about Hang Wood are complex. What does he like about it, and what makes him afraid?

CHAPTER 9   Waking at dawn the next morning, the boys feel a sense of contentment in the wood. Hooper watches a thrush as it eats a snail, and Kingshaw goes to swim in the stream.

They hear dogs approaching and realise that a search party has found them.

Entirely at ease in the wood, Kingshaw initially dreads returning to Warings, but he reassures himself that things have changed.

COMMENT   This short chapter epitomises Kingshaw's feelings about the environment of the wood. With daylight, its innocence is restored. Hooper watches the thrush and mildly argues about feeding it. Kingshaw lies in the stream absorbing the tranquillity and beauty of the scene. All is well until the crashing sound of approaching people breaks the spell.

The closing account of the episode in Hang Wood leaves an idyllic impression on the reader, and heightens the contrast in Kingshaw's mind between this environment and that of Warings.

GLOSSARY   **watered silk** a silk fabric on which a wavy pattern has been produced

A — *What do these quotations describe?*

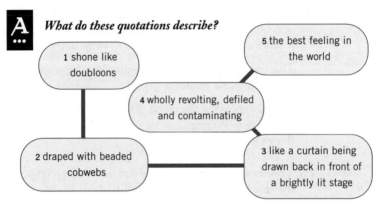

1 shone like doubloons

2 draped with beaded cobwebs

4 wholly revolting, defiled and contaminating

5 the best feeling in the world

3 like a curtain being drawn back in front of a brightly lit stage

Who says or thinks the following?

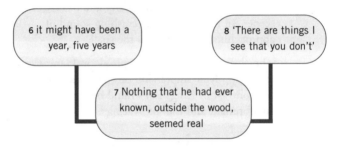

6 it might have been a year, five years

8 'There are things I see that you don't'

7 Nothing that he had ever known, outside the wood, seemed real

Check your answers on page 78.

B — *Consider these issues.*

a How and why the author creates an impression of a longer period of time when only one day and night passes in the wood.

b The descriptive qualities of the language in this section, and how the author creates a vivid sense of place.

c Kingshaw's perception of the way power shifts between him and Hooper.

d New aspects of the characters of the boys shown in this section.

e The difference in the type of fear felt by Kingshaw and Hooper.

f The author's use of colloquial (see Literary Terms) phrases, typical of young boys' speech.

CHAPTER 10

Back at Warings, Hooper persuades his father and Mrs Kingshaw that Kingshaw pushed him into the water, causing the bruise on his head.

Kingshaw's frustration at their acceptance of Hooper's lies drives him to fury. He feels remote from both adults and increasingly isolated.

What is meant by Mrs Kingshaw's 'way of speaking to Mr Hooper'? (p. 114)

Afraid of favouring her own son, Mrs Kingshaw pampers Hooper. Kingshaw feels ashamed of her anxiety to please.

Kingshaw is sent to his room, where he reflects on the futility of his own actions in the face of Hooper's power. When his mother comes to say goodnight, they talk about Hang Wood and Hooper.

Before she leaves him, Mrs Kingshaw hints at an important piece of news that he will be told tomorrow. Kingshaw dreads the announcement of her marriage to Mr Hooper.

Kingshaw concludes that he can have no confidence in other people, only in 'things and places'. He thinks about the wood for a long time before going to bed.

COMMENT

Reading Hooper's words in the opening paragraph of this chapter, we see his power reasserted at Warings.

Kingshaw is driven to isolation. His torment intensifies when even the adults appear to align themselves with Hooper. The author shows his hopelessness and frustration through descriptions of their 'blank faces', and Kingshaw's feelings that 'it was like having a wall in front of him which he must batter down'. He feels 'locked up in himself', trapped by this house which is 'taking over again'.

THE RETURN TO WARINGS

Look at how the references to Mrs Kingshaw's jewellery and make-up are used to emphasise her remoteness from her son, as well as, perhaps, her new role as the prospective wife of Mr Hooper.

Hang Wood, and in particular the stream, come into Kingshaw's thoughts repeatedly. He appears to regard it as a possible escape, but there are undertones of potential danger in his paradoxical (see Literary Terms) description of the wood as 'Terrifying and safe'.

CHAPTER 11

At breakfast the next morning, Mr Hooper announces that the adults have decided that Charles will join Edmund at his school in the new term, instead of returning to St Vincent's.

Kingshaw is panic-stricken and has to escape from Hooper and the house. He runs out of the grounds to some allotments where there is a deserted shed in which he hides. Almost immediately, the door slams and he is locked in.

Note how the description of Kingshaw's nightmare contributes to our understanding of his character.

For a while there is silence outside. Although Kingshaw suspects that Hooper has locked him in, his fearful mind turns to other possibilities, fuelled by horror stories that he has read at school. Thoughts of school bring on his dread of going to school with Hooper, until his panic and terror make him vomit. Eventually he falls asleep.

He is roused from a nightmare by Hooper, who torments him from the outside of the shed, playing on Kingshaw's fears of moths and other creatures, and threatening further torments when they are both at the same school.

Hooper goes away, leaving him in the shed. Broken by his persecution, Kingshaw weeps uncontrollably. Eventually, Hooper returns. He blithely unlocks the door and returns to the house, where he tells Mrs Kingshaw that they have been playing bandits.

COMMENT

This chilling episode marks a new level of sophistication in Hooper's persecution of Kingshaw:

What is the symbolic significance of Hooper washing his hands?

- He finds Kingshaw in a place which he considered safe
- When he locks the door, he is silent. He leaves Kingshaw alone in the darkness to weaken him and demonstrate his own control
- On his return, he rekindles Kingshaw's known fears and plays on them
- He threatens Kingshaw with further torment in the future
- He almost succeeds in breaking Kingshaw's spirit, reducing him to utter hopelessness
- His behaviour remains undiscovered because Kingshaw's mother, who should protect her son, makes only the most superficial enquiry about what they have been doing

Features of Kingshaw's nightmare are based on his experience and his fears. He feels isolated and frightened in spite of being amongst a large crowd. We are reminded that Kingshaw now feels that people cannot help him. Even his friend Devereux is unresponsive. The ghastly memory of the crow is revived, and what should have been an innocent entertainment is distorted into horror.

GLOSSARY

Punch and Judy a traditional puppet show which presents the violent fights between Mr Punch and his wife Judy in an amusing way

dorm abbreviation for 'dormitory', the shared bedroom in a boarding school

CHAPTER **12**

The boys and their parents go for a day out to Leydell Castle.

What mixture of feelings does Kingshaw experience at the top of the castle?

Kingshaw, confident and sure-footed, decides to climb the ruined walls. Hooper watches him from below, and reveals that he is afraid of heights. Kingshaw feels exhilarated and free from his parents and Hooper. He dares Hooper to climb the wall. A few minutes later, he sees that Hooper has climbed up to a narrow ledge where he is now stuck, paralysed by his fear of heights.

Kingshaw goes to help him. Unable to pass Hooper on the narrow ledge, he tries to guide him down by telling him what to do, but Hooper is too afraid to follow his instructions. Kingshaw notices that Hooper has wet himself in fear. He feels again a temporary thrill of power over his tormentor, but experience has taught him that it cannot last beyond the immediate situation. He feels that here he is 'King of the Castle', but, in spite of his hatred, he will not do anything to harm Hooper.

As he reaches out to take hold of Hooper and guide him, Hooper flinches and falls off the ledge.

COMMENT
On this 'family' outing the parents are shown to be absorbed in each other, and still ignorant of the relationship between their sons.

Away from Warings, in a new environment, Kingshaw is again seen to be more confident and resourceful than Hooper.

We see where the title of the novel comes from. An innocent children's rhyme is given more sinister overtones when seen against the background of Hooper's relentless torment and Kingshaw's helpless hatred. It is an example of the darker aspects of childhood which Susan Hill explores in this novel.

Our sympathy for Kingshaw is aroused when Hooper falls. After Hooper's successful lies about his fall into the stream, we realise that Kingshaw will inevitably be blamed for this incident as well.

GLOSSARY
I'm the King of the Castle the first line of a traditional children's rhyme 'I'm the king of the castle, and you're the dirty rascal'

CHAPTER 13

Ignored by the adults, and overcome with guilt at having thought about pushing Hooper off the ledge, Kingshaw believes that Hooper has died. He feels that the accident inevitably followed his own wish that Hooper should fall, even though he had genuinely reached out to help him.

Thoughts of death prompt a flashback to a scene from school assembly, in which an unpleasant boy called Lesage reads a text about the soul leaving the body.

Mrs Kingshaw drives her son back to Warings in the Hoopers' car. She does not to speak to him. Unable to bear the silence, Kingshaw tries to tell her what really happened on the ledge. She responds with mild

reproach, and dismisses his explanation. At Warings she
hugs him and asks him to promise not to do anything
so dangerous again. Kingshaw feels no affection in her
embrace, only alarm at her unusually urgent expression.

Kingshaw is left at Warings under the supervision of
Mrs Boland, the daily help, while his mother returns to
the hospital to see Hooper. Mrs Boland is watching
television when Kingshaw comes to her room. He is
frightened by a scene on television which is full of
suspense when a blind man is secretly followed. He
leaves the room, but still hears the terrible sound of
someone screaming. He goes to bed frightened, but
comforts himself with the thought that, following
Hooper's death, he might be allowed to return to the
security of St Vincent's, instead of being sent to a new
school.

Kingshaw wakes from a nightmare. He is so afraid that
he goes to find his mother, instead of forcing himself to
wait until the fear passes in his usual independent way.
He panics when he finds her room empty, thinking that
he must be alone in the house. He is crying on the
landing when Mr Hooper runs upstairs, lifts him and
Look at what this carries him to his mother in the sitting room. They tell
chapter shows about him that Hooper is not dead.
the relationship
between Mr Mr Hooper carries him back to bed, and Kingshaw is
Hooper and Mrs ashamed of having felt comforted in his arms. He
Kingshaw. wakes in the night with the thought that Hooper is still
alive, and it is some time before he goes back to sleep.

C OMMENT Kingshaw's superstitious fear is shown again when he
compares Hooper's fall with the transfer of warts from
another boy to himself.

The flashback to events at school, and the strange
behaviour of Lesage towards Kingshaw, reminds us that
Kingshaw has been bullied before, even at St Vincent's.
In the past he was always able to defend himself. The

What might be the significance of the description of Kingshaw's reflection in the mirror 'as though in water'?

fact that none of Kingshaw's strategies work against Hooper, is a reflection of the power and more evil nature of his persecution.

Images (see Literary Terms) of the surrounding countryside create a hostile atmosphere around Kingshaw – the rumbling thunder, the snaky tree roots, and the monstrous combine harvester.

Can you link the images in his nightmare to Kingshaw's fears and memories of recent events?

A *'To whom' or 'what' do these quotations refer?*

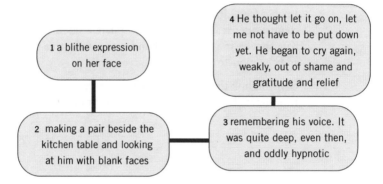

> 1 a blithe expression on her face

> 4 He thought let it go on, let me not have to be put down yet. He began to cry again, weakly, out of shame and gratitude and relief

> 2 making a pair beside the kitchen table and looking at him with blank faces

> 3 remembering his voice. It was quite deep, even then, and oddly hypnotic

Identify the speaker.

> 5 I am the king, there is nothing I can't ask him for, nothing he won't promise me, nothing I can't do to him

Check your answers on page 78.

 B *Consider these issues.*

a The evidence of the developing relationship between Mr Hooper and Mrs Kingshaw.

b The author's use of Kingshaw's nightmares to provide insight into his fears and his character.

c The nature of Mrs Kingshaw's speech, her appearance and her behaviour towards her son.

d The accumulation of references to Hang Wood, and more particularly the stream, as a place of refuge.

e The purpose in the novel of the trip to Leydell Castle.

f How the author develops our awareness of Kingshaw's isolation.

g Kingshaw's mixed feelings after Hooper's fall.

CHAPTER **14**

A week later, Kingshaw is left at Warings when Mr Hooper goes to London and Mrs Kingshaw goes to visit Hooper in hospital. His mother asks him to buy a present for Hooper, but he reacts furiously, telling her again how much he hates him.

He reflects on his feelings of embarrassment about the way his mother has fussed around him since the accident, and compares himself to a boy called Fenwick at school who refused to let anyone pamper him after a bad fall. He has tried to be like Fenwick, but believes that the events of the summer have proved him to be a failure and a coward.

During the previous week, happy in his own company, he has made a helter-skelter model. He is proud that it has turned out well.

He borrows a jigsaw from Hooper's room, but puts it back, regretting that he ever went in there, and feeling that Hooper will inevitably realise that he did.

He goes out and walks along the lane, then decides to go into the church. Standing on the altar, he is overcome with fear of the consequences of his hateful feelings towards Hooper. He kneels and tries to pray, telling God that he did not really want Hooper to die, but knowing that God will know the truth. He recognises that his fear of Hooper is greater than his fear of anything else.

Susan Hill makes Fielding seem like a normal, uncomplicated boy.

He is praying desperately for help when a boy comes up to him. At first Kingshaw is suspicious and afraid of another stranger, but when they go outside, the boy, Fielding, draws him into a game and he begins to enjoy himself.

y

SUICIDE – THE ONLY ANSWER

Fielding lives at a neighbouring farm. He takes
Kingshaw to see a calf being born, then shows him
some young turkeys and his pet hamster. He invites
Kingshaw to stay for dinner. When Kingshaw returns
to Warings to ask his mother's permission, she tells him
that Hooper will be coming home the next day.

Kingshaw tells Fielding about Hooper's treatment of
him, and his own terrible fear, but Fielding cannot
properly understand him. He advises Kingshaw to stand
up for himself, and regards his problems with Hooper
in a matter-of-fact way.

They go together to a ditch to look for slow-worms,
and Kingshaw stumbles across Fielding's lost tortoise.
He is proud and happy when Fielding praises him for
finding it. He decides that Fielding will be his own
friend, and the thought gives him confidence.

Kingshaw is delighted the next day when Hooper is not
well enough to come home from hospital. He goes to
see Fielding, and decides that everything will be all
right if he can learn to be like him in every way.

COMMENT   Kingshaw's troubled character and fears are emphasised
through contrast with Fielding's easy friendliness and
self-confidence.

The isolation and confinement of Warings is shown
when Kingshaw does not know Fielding, yet Fielding
seems to know a lot about him.

This is an interlude of happiness for Kingshaw. With
Hooper away in hospital, he can escape from Warings
to be with his own friend.

The birth of the calf, and the presence and warmth of
the animals, are symbols of life at Fielding's farm. They
provide a strong contrast with the symbols of death
which the author has associated with Warings.

The contrast between Warings and Fielding's home is further illustrated by Fielding's mother. With her unadorned appearance and natural manner, she seems to be all that Kingshaw's mother is not.

Hooper appears in this chapter only in a brief paragraph which shows his calculating nature and spiteful attitude in relation to Mrs Kingshaw's visits.

GLOSSARY

Dettol the brand name of an antiseptic liquid used to clean Fenwick's wound

brazened it out faced up to people boldly, making them accept his lies or overlook his behaviour

CHAPTER 15

When Hooper returns from hospital, he guesses about the jigsaw and calls Kingshaw a thief. Kingshaw's mother is anxious that he should spend time with Hooper. She ignores him when he tells her his feelings, believing that he is going through a silly phase.

Hooper taunts Kingshaw, boasting about the gifts that Mrs Kingshaw brought to him in hospital, and blaming him for the accident. He threatens retribution, and Kingshaw dreads his plans.

Kingshaw compares Hooper's persecution with the physical bullying he experienced at the hands of a boy called Crawford at school.

To escape the house, he decides to go to Fielding's, telling his mother that he is going to buy an ice cream.

As he stands on the bridge eating his ice cream, Fielding drives past with his father in their Land Rover. They invite Kingshaw to go with them to market where they will sell the heifer calf. Kingshaw is upset by Mr Fielding's casual statement that it will be sold for veal.

He returns to Warings and Mrs Kingshaw sends him up to sit with Hooper. Hooper reveals that he knows about Fielding.

What does
Kingshaw mean
when he thinks 'it
had all begun'?

Mr Hooper takes Kingshaw to London to buy his uniform for the new term at Hooper's school. Dressed in the strange clothes, Kingshaw feels a sense of hopelessness.

Back at Warings, Kingshaw is furious to find that Hooper has been allowed to play with his helter-skelter model. Almost hysterically he shouts at the adults until Mr Hooper slaps him across the face. Mrs Kingshaw sends him to his room.

He goes upstairs and bursts into Hooper's room to get his model back. Hooper is triumphant. As Kingshaw lunges forward to punch him, Hooper throws the model across the room and breaks it.

Mrs Kingshaw, who has followed him upstairs, says only that her son should be ashamed of himself.

COMMENT   Consider how Kingshaw's isolation from the other characters, especially his mother, is shown in this chapter. She cares anxiously for Hooper and ignores her own son's feelings. The adults appear to have adopted a firm approach to Kingshaw, yet remain unaware of Hooper's lies and bullying. His isolation is emphasised when even the Fieldings drive off, and he walks back to Warings alone.

You should decide whether Kingshaw is more moral than Hooper, or simply more afraid of the consequences of his actions. When he 'broke out into a cold sweat, at his own wickedness' (p. 165), was it conscience or fear that affected him?

The adults' way of speaking makes them appear remote and less real than the boys. Kingshaw is aware of his mother's artificial language, 'He squirmed, hating the way she spoke of herself like that, as though she were another person' (p. 168). What other features of their speech have you noticed?

Kingshaw has confused feelings about Mr Hooper. He sees his mother trying to please him and realises, with some resentment, Mr Hooper's influence on their lives. He is still ashamed of the sense of security he had in Mr Hooper's arms.

Kingshaw believes that the calf represents the link between himself and the Fieldings. It is significant that immediately after it is taken away to market, his secret pleasure in his new friend is spoiled when Hooper reveals that he knows about Fielding.

CHAPTER 16

Mrs Kingshaw receives a phone call from a friend. Mr Hooper listens to her conversation, resentful that she has friends from before her time at Warings. Knowing that Mr Hooper is listening, Mrs Kingshaw says that she has not yet made plans for the future. By suggesting that she might leave Warings, she hopes to prompt Mr Hooper to propose to her.

Mrs Kingshaw's plan has the desired effect. Mr Hooper feels anxious at the prospect of her leaving. He reflects guiltily on the strength of his sexual desires, and his unsatisfactory relationship with his first wife. He believes that with Mrs Kingshaw as his wife his needs would be satisfied. Afraid of being left alone again, he resolves to propose to her the next day.

Kingshaw also hears what his mother says. He is confused by her hints that they might leave Warings, after so much has been done to prepare for his change of school. He remembers other places in which they have lived, the worst being a private hotel where he was troubled by the presence of an old woman called Miss Mellitt.

Hooper tells him the news that their parents will be married before the start of the new term. Kingshaw realises that Hooper is angry, yet unable to prevent this permanent invasion of his house. Kingshaw himself is deeply upset. He wakes in the night and weeps at the thought of his future at Warings.

Note how the description of the circus gives a vivid picture of Kingshaw's fear.

The adults arrange a surprise outing to the circus. Mrs Kingshaw knows that her son was afraid of a circus when he was younger, but she dismisses his fears as childish. Kingshaw suffers through the performance, hating the smells and terrified that the huge tent will collapse around them. At the end of the performance, on the way out, he is violently sick.

Mrs Kingshaw announces that she has called at the Fieldings' farm to invite Fielding to tea. Kingshaw is angry that she has intruded on his special friendship, and worried that the friendship will be spoiled when Fielding meets Hooper.

The wedding of Mrs Kingshaw and Mr Hooper has been arranged for 10th September. It will be held in the morning, and the boys will be taken to school in the afternoon, following a celebratory 'family' lunch.

When Fielding comes to Warings, Hooper takes over, deciding what they should do and trying to impress him. He shows off the moths in the Red Room and suggests that they go up to the attics where the stuffed crow is kept, knowing that this will reveal Kingshaw's fears and perhaps undermine his friendship with Fielding.

Kingshaw admires Fielding's self-confident behaviour. He sees that Fielding's candid responses and lack of fear mean that Hooper accepts what he says and can exert no power over him.

Aware of Kingshaw's discomfort, Fielding turns away from the attics and suggests instead that they all go to his farm. Hooper is eager to go, but Kingshaw refuses. The farm is spoiled for him now by Hooper's intrusion in what he considered his own place.

Fielding is puzzled by Kingshaw's behaviour and wants to go back for him. Hooper persuades him that Kingshaw is moody, and will follow them later, so they go to the farm without him.

When they have gone, Kingshaw goes to Hooper's room and removes all the battle plans and maps. He takes them to the clearing and burns them. With a sense of foreboding, he realises that Hooper will know, and he tries to put out of his mind that only five days remain until 10th September.

COMMENT   It is ironic (see Literary Terms) that Mrs Kingshaw reflects on the safety of Warings at the beginning of this chapter. What do her thoughts reveal about her character?

Although Mrs Kingshaw and Mr Hooper are deliberately undeveloped characters, the author does give some important details about them. What are their reasons for marriage, and how do they regard each other?

This chapter shows more of Fielding's character. He is puzzled by Hooper's boasts and Kingshaw's unresponsive behaviour. His presence emphasises the characters of the other boys, and the tensions between them.

Kingshaw's recognition that Fielding is comfortable with anybody, and prepared even to enjoy being with Hooper, makes him feel disappointed in his friend. He decides again that he can rely only on himself, and tells himself that he has 'finished' with Fielding. His isolation is emphasised when Fielding goes off with Hooper.

GLOSSARY   **odd straws in the wind** hints or signs of some future event

CHAPTER 17

On 9th September there is a sense of anticipation as the trunks are packed and final preparations made for the wedding, and the boys' return to school.

Kingshaw regards the activity in a remote way, concerned only with his fear of what is to come. Hooper has said nothing to him about the disappearance of the things from his room, and Kingshaw dreads the thought of Hooper's retribution and the terror of his future at school.

That night Hooper pushes a note under Kingshaw's door warning that something will happen to him. The power of the threat brings on Kingshaw's nightmares.

Why has Susan Hill juxtaposed the account of Kingshaw's actions with references to other characters at Warings?

He wakes at dawn. Remembering the other dawn when he escaped to Hang Wood, he is drawn back to the peace he found there. He goes to the stream. Almost in a trance, and thinking of all that has happened, he hesitates only briefly before lying face down in it, and deliberately drowning himself.

Hooper leads the search party, knowing where Kingshaw would go. When he sees the body in the water, he is triumphant at having driven his victim to suicide.

The novel ends with the image of Mrs Kingshaw comforting Hooper, as men splash through the water to bring out her dead son.

COMMENT   Earlier in the novel, Kingshaw clung to the hope that he could escape or survive Hooper's persecution, but Hooper's methods have been so successful that he now lives in hopeless fear of certain misery at home and at school.

The ironic final image (see Literary Terms) of the novel – of Mrs Kingshaw comforting her son's persecutor – is a damning reflection of her blindness, and the triumphant conclusion of Hooper's plans.

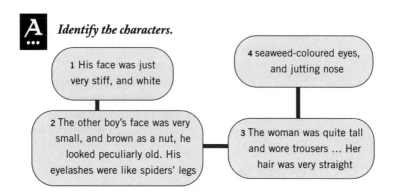

A *Identify the characters.*

1 His face was just very stiff, and white

4 seaweed-coloured eyes, and jutting nose

2 The other boy's face was very small, and brown as a nut, he looked peculiarly old. His eyelashes were like spiders' legs

3 The woman was quite tall and wore trousers ... Her hair was very straight

'To whom' does this quotation refer?

5 He had thought that he couldn't be afraid of anything again, but now he was afraid

Check your answers on page 78.

B *Consider these issues.*

a What is shown of Kingshaw's character by his thoughts about Fenwick's bravery.

b Kingshaw's confused attitude towards God and religion.

c Fielding's character and role in the novel.

d Kingshaw's opinion on the differences between Mrs Fielding and his own mother.

e The contrast in the atmosphere of Warings and the Fieldings' farm.

f The reasons behind Kingshaw's complete loss of hope at the end of the novel.

g Hooper's feelings at the end of the novel.

PART THREE

COMMENTARY

THEMES

CHILDHOOD In her introduction, Susan Hill explains the source of this novel's central theme: she is fascinated by the subject of childhood. Her interest is in finding the truth about childhood experience, and presenting it to adults to help them to understand it better. Therefore, this book was written for adults, even though it tells the story of two young boys.

From the beginning of the novel, we are shown how childhood experience forms an individual's character, and has a lasting influence in later life. Mr Hooper returns repeatedly to his past, using his unhappy childhood as the explanation for present problems. The lack of love in Hooper's childhood goes some way to explaining his callous behaviour, whilst Kingshaw's fearfulness and uncertainty is directly linked to the insecurity of his family life.

The novel challenges adults' beliefs that children are resilient and happy. By drawing clear parallels between Hooper and Kingshaw – both only children, both with one parent, similar in age and social background – Susan Hill suggests that any situation can have a number of unhappy outcomes for children.

Which aspects of Kingshaw's life have influenced his character and behaviour?

Kingshaw and Hooper are treated seriously. Kingshaw's sensitivity and awareness of others show more complexity than we might expect in a ten-year-old. His feelings are as intense as an adult's, but childhood powerlessness is emphasised when no-one understands him, and important decisions about his home and school are made without consultation by the adults around him. In Hooper, we have to face the disturbing truth that evil can exist in a child of his age. This raises questions about a child's responsibility for its actions.

Find some
examples of the
adults' insensitive
behaviour towards
the boys.

The novel criticises adults' insensitivity and misinterpretation of children's feelings by showing the reader that Mrs Kingshaw and Mr Hooper must share the blame with Hooper for Kingshaw's suicide. Our own ability to understand is challenged by the shocking conclusion. The success of the novel is that the ending is so believable: we are left in no doubt that Kingshaw could see no other means of escape. It would be easy to think that this would not happen in real life, but we have to accept that it sometimes does.

In spite of its concentration on the cruelty and isolation of childhood, the novel is not entirely pessimistic. Some readers will recognise elements of their own experience in the events described, or will know of children who have been persecuted by bullies. However, Kingshaw's suffering and Hooper's extreme cruelty are particular to these characters. In her introduction, Susan Hill describes them as 'misfits' – theirs is not the experience of most children. The isolation of Warings sets the events apart from ordinary life. Only Fielding's character and family provide a reassuring reminder that children can be happy and understood. The tragic combination of the Kingshaws and Hoopers at Warings is not a bleak reflection of all children's experience, but a challenge to readers to reconsider perceptions of childhood, and the responsibilities of adults towards children in their care.

ISOLATION AND THE LACK OF LOVE

Isolation in
family
relationships

The four main characters in the novel are remarkable for the lack of love in their lives. None of them loves another person, or experiences the enhancing effects of being loved by someone else. In spite of being forced into close proximity – as only children with widowed parents – they are isolated characters, unable to relate to others – even in their families.

In the Hooper family there is a history of cold, unaffectionate relationships, from the old Mr Hooper's authoritative rule to Edmund's contemptuous detachment from his father. Mr Hooper did not love his wife, who was cold and reserved. Contemplating marriage to Mrs Kingshaw, he looks forward only to sexual gratification, with little thought of mutual affection or esteem.

Does Susan Hill suggest reasons for the adults' misunderstanding of their sons?

Mrs Kingshaw is incapable of loving her son. She leads a superficial life, concerned with appearances and material security. Her displays of affection are embarrassing to Kingshaw, and he realises that they lack the warmth of love and understanding. Kingshaw alone shows a sensitivity which suggests that he has the capacity to love, but with no example to follow he has become guarded and uncertain.

The effect of the lack of love on characters is the important point. Susan Hill sees love as an empowering emotion: people flourish in loving relationships which foster their confidence and create a deep source of happiness which they are able to share with others. Fielding, who comes from a loving family, shares his confidence and happiness with those he meets. We see Kingshaw at his most relaxed when he plays battleships with Fielding. Even Hooper is baffled into accepting Fielding's way of behaviour when Fielding comes to tea at Warings.

The benefits of love

The other characters are debilitated by the lack of love in their lives. It undermines their confidence and their relationships, resulting in isolation. The absence of love has the most disturbing effect on Hooper, in whom there is an emotional vacuum, and therefore nothing to counter the evil that possesses him.

The novel emphasises that characters are forced into isolation by the lack of love in their lives. By recording their thoughts, Susan Hill gives an insight into their inability to relate to other people, or understand their motives and behaviour. In Chapter 16, when Mrs Kingshaw speaks to her friend on the phone, we see how she and Mr Hooper are unable to communicate frankly with each other.

Why is Kingshaw seen to experience a wider range of emotions than Hooper?

Most isolated of all is Kingshaw. The adults maintain their indifference to his suffering throughout the story, in spite of his efforts to make them understand. The hope he places in a return to his own school, and then in Fielding, is destroyed. In Chapter 16, already close to despair, he sees his mother's lack of love as an active force against him, as she discusses with Mr Hooper the future of the moth collection.

Isolated setting The theme of isolation is reinforced through the description of the setting and natural environment. Warings stands alone, isolated from the village of Derne. When Kingshaw ventures into the surrounding countryside there are hostile images to emphasise his loneliness and vulnerability: the crow is the most memorable, but there is also the deserted landscape as he makes his way to Hang Wood in Chapter 5, and the hostility of the countryside in Chapter 13.

Kingshaw had sufficient insight to recognise the lack of love in his life, but the others are less sensitive, unable to comprehend such feelings, even when faced with Kingshaw's death.

CRUELTY AND THE POWER OF EVIL

A vein of cruelty runs through the novel, suggesting the underlying presence of danger and sinister influences. At its strongest it is represented by Hooper's treatment of Kingshaw, but it is present in other more subtle ways. Starting with the collection of moths in the Red Room, it is frequently associated with animals such as the predatory crow, the thrush banging open a snail's shell, the killing of turkeys on Fielding's farm and the humiliation of elephants in the circus. The widespread cruelty of childhood is shown through Kingshaw's reflections on his encounters with other boys.

The novel shows us what might happen when a child does not learn these values.

Cruelty is not unusual in children. In the struggle to survive as part of a group, the weakest are often oppressed, but society seeks to correct the balance and preserve the safety of even its weakest members. Cruel behaviour in children is corrected, and the values of love and compassion are taught.

Hooper has suffered the kinds of experience which could explain his social problems: his mother died, he is unloved by his father and he is jealous of the arrival in his home of another boy. It is clear that love and compassion have played little part in his young life. But other children have these experiences and survive them. Another explanation for his behaviour could be that he has been influenced by some evil force. There are hints of strangeness in the description of Hooper – references to something unusual in his eyes and a sense of mystery about his personality. In the absence of love, darker feelings have been allowed to develop, and are given free rein in a boy who has never been adequately guided.

It is disturbing at the end of the novel to confront the fact that Hooper's evil has triumphed over good, and all the more disturbing because Hooper is only a child. We are made to consider our belief in the innocence of childhood and question the source of his evil power. The evil power remains a mystery, beyond our understanding inside Edmund Hooper's mind, but the evidence of its existence is clear, in his sense of triumph at Kingshaw's death.

STRUCTURE

EPISODES The novel tells the story of Kingshaw and Hooper in a series of episodes, interspersed with accounts of past experience. The sections describing the boys together are sharply focused on the most significant interaction between them. There are few distractions in the way of references to the details of ordinary life, because Kingshaw's suffering is the principal concern. The vivid portrayal of these events reflects their place at the front of Kingshaw's mind. Susan Hill creates an impression of the cumulative nature of Hooper's persecution, and Kingshaw's fear, by describing the incidents separately and emphasising how neither change of place to Hang Wood, nor the influence of other people such as Fielding, can make any improvement to their relationship.

FLASHBACK The main events take place during the short period of the summer holidays, but if you consider the novel carefully you will see that much of it deals with the past – the time before the Kingshaws' arrival at Warings. This technique of bringing the past into the story is called 'flashback'. Most readers will be familiar with the use of this device from film and television, but there is also a literary tradition of telling a story in this way. It allows the author to select and emphasise particular features, and present events from the point of view of different narrators. By allowing individual characters to use their own voices to recount experiences, the author provides insight into their thoughts and feelings, and shows how their lives have been shaped and influenced.

CHARACTERS' THOUGHTS

How do Mr Hooper's thoughts show his limited understanding of people and relationships?

In this novel it is significant which characters' memories and thoughts are recorded. Kingshaw reflects most on past experience, promoting our understanding and arousing our sympathy for him. To a smaller extent, Mr Hooper also thinks about the past. The flashback to his childhood, and the account of his unspoken thoughts early in the novel, contribute to the setting of the scene and our understanding of the potential problems in Edmund's character. Later, his thoughts about his unhappy marriage reveal more of Mr Hooper's character which leads us to understand, and perhaps to sympathise, with some of his problems. Mrs Kingshaw is too shallow to reflect on the past: her concern is with securing her happiness in the future. The absence of Hooper's thoughts and memories reflects his lack of conscience, and maintains the inscrutability of his character.

It is important to see the author's decision about structure (see Literary Terms) as a deliberate one, based on her purpose in writing the novel. In this novel about childhood the episodic (see Literary Terms) narrative reflects a boy's view of the events which overwhelm him. His introspective thoughts and memories convince us of his isolation, and persuade us to believe that suicide is his only means of escape.

CHARACTERS

EDMUND HOOPER

Background

*Unloved and
unlovable
Scheming
Malevolent
Wholly without
conscience*

Susan Hill's portrayal of Hooper's malevolent bullying forces us to consider the sources of his behaviour. Is he a naturally evil boy, or the shocking product of his family circumstances?

His own father finds him disturbing. His thoughts about his son early in the novel reveal that Edmund is cold and inscrutable, a difficult child to love. Later, comparing Edmund with Charles Kingshaw, Mr Hooper thinks that his son has always been strange. However, we must consider the reliability of his assessment of Edmund against what we know of Mr Hooper's poor judgement and capacity for self-deception. With more detachment, the reader can see how Mr Hooper's own unhappy childhood, his failed marriage and general inadequacies must have been important influences in shaping Edmund's character. Although his mother, who died six years ago, had the knack of dealing with Hooper, we are given no impression of a loving relationship between mother and son. Hooper barely remembers her. Significantly, he cannot imagine which aspects of a mother's presence he might be expected to miss.

Relationships

Hooper is an isolated only child. His hobbies, such as the preparation of battle plans, are solitary and devoid of human involvement. He has no friends, unlike Kingshaw who thinks of Devereux and plays comfortably with Fielding. Hooper relates to other boys only by trying to control them.

One reason, perhaps, for his inability to relate normally to people lies in his watchful approach to others. He is smaller than Kingshaw but he seems older, more aware and calculating. He is detached and unresponsive towards his father, who is disturbed by Edmund's knowing looks and uncomfortable questions. Later, his awareness of worldly affairs, and his observation of Mrs Kingshaw's behaviour alert him to the likelihood of her marriage to Mr Hooper.

His instinctive detection and understanding of fear is his starting point in relationships with other boys: he weighs up their characters to see if he can gain control. Fielding baffles him by his easy confidence, but Hooper soon realises that Kingshaw is an easy victim. Hooper's own strong fears of things like the storm and being lost in the wood, are quickly put behind him, whereas Kingshaw is vulnerable because he carries his fears with him and magnifies them in his mind.

An evil boy?   At the beginning, Hooper appears to bully Kingshaw as an experiment to satisfy his curiosity about Kingshaw's behaviour when afraid, but he soon displays a malevolent enjoyment of his power to control. He approaches the persecution with cold deliberation, delighting in his plans and showing no scruples about the suffering he inflicts.

An important aspect of Hooper's character is his lack of conscience. He is contemptuous of his father's feeble attempt to guide his behaviour towards Kingshaw, and we are given the impression of an inadequate parent who has failed in his duty to develop his son's sense of morality and compassion. Mr Hooper's own family pride is the example and foundation for Edmund's snobbishness and superiority towards the impoverished Kingshaws. Other moral influences have made little impression on him. In his conversation about death with Kingshaw, he dismisses religious teaching as 'guff'.

The author explores at length Kingshaw's complex feelings of hatred, guilt and responsibility towards Hooper, but we are never given such insight into

Hooper's thoughts – perhaps because Hooper never reflects on his own behaviour and its consequences. At the end of the novel, as Kingshaw leaves the house, Hooper enjoys untroubled sleep, his mind 'blank' in spite of all the damage he has done. The strongest suggestion of an evil nature is his lack of remorse at the end, when he feels only triumph at his victim's death.

Do you feel any sympathy for Edmund Hooper? Why?

The depiction of his character is made more disturbing by the reminders that Hooper is only a ten-year-old boy: he puts his tongue out when he is concentrating on colouring a map, and enjoys the monster story which he reads on the train. His fears of the storm and of being lost are typically childish. These details force the reader to look at Hooper as a child, monstrous though he might seem. He is a child who has known no love or firm guidance and in whom, for whatever reason, a vacuum exists where there should be compassion and human feeling.

On Kingshaw's arrival, he feels resentment and anger, followed by a delight in the exercise of power. These are normal feelings, but in Hooper they are the starting point for the abnormally cruel behaviour which results in Kingshaw's death. Susan Hill deliberately does not define Hooper's motives: his unrestrained, remorseless behaviour, and its frightening, tragic consequences are made all the more evil because we cannot understand their source. The character of Edmund Hooper is a warning that such evil can exist, and his family background an example of the circumstances in which it can thrive.

CHARLES KINGSHAW

If Hooper represents the power of evil, Charles Kingshaw might be seen as his good and innocent victim. By exploring Kingshaw's feelings, and relating much of the action through his eyes, Susan Hill makes us sympathise with him, and feel the horror of Hooper's persecution. Knowing Kingshaw well, we understand why he is so vulnerable, and believe in his suicide as the inevitable conclusion of his suffering.

Kingshaw is ginger haired and taller than Hooper. He is an unremarkable boy, in both appearance and achievement. At school he maintains his anonymity by being academically average and indistinguishable from many other boys.

Relationships and self-esteem   Like Hooper, he observes other people closely, but unlike Hooper he has low self-esteem and constantly measures his own shortcomings against their behaviour and confidence. His expectation that others are stronger or more successful has produced in him a fatalistic approach to life. He is resigned to being disappointed and to things working out badly.

It is debatable whether Kingshaw's preoccupation with his own inadequacies is the result, or the cause, of his problems in relating to other boys. In spite of his feelings of inadequacy, he does have friends: Devereux has invited him to spend the holiday with his family, and he joins in naturally with Fielding's game of battleships. His anxiety about coping with other boys reflects his confusing and unhappy experiences, which Susan Hill relates for the reader through the flashback technique (see Structure): incidents such as Turville's dares at the swimming pool, Broughton-Smith's warts and Fenwick's bravery, are plausible to the reader and represent for Kingshaw the attitudes and behaviour of 'normal' boys. Kingshaw does not feel normal, and in

Fearful
Sensitive
Insecure
Isolated from
other people
Forced himself
into
independence

Why does
Kingshaw feel
happier at school?

her introduction to the novel, Susan Hill describes him as a misfit.

He displays certain qualities throughout the novel, such as practical skills in making the helter-skelter model, and his resourcefulness in Hang Wood. He sometimes allows himself to feel proud of his achievements – like being the only boy to have climbed over the school buildings to the top of a tree, and coping better than Hooper in Hang Wood. However, these feelings of self-congratulation are short-lived. Kingshaw's habitual feelings of fear and doubt always take over again.

The main cause of Kingshaw's insecurity is his unhappy family background. He keeps a photograph of his father, who died a few years earlier, but there are no affectionate associations with him, only a little pride that he had been a pilot in the Battle of Britain. Kingshaw has never missed him and does not even know exactly when his father died. Since his father's death, the Kingshaws' life has been difficult. Several references are made to the places in which they have lived, and it is likely that the series of private hotels with strange inhabitants, like Miss Mellitt, have contributed to Kingshaw's insecurity.

Kingshaw's relationship with his mother is uncomfortable. He is embarrassed by her efforts to keep up appearances and by her artificial shows of affection. Away from her and his home, he regards his school as a haven of security. In Chapter 3, we are shown how firmly he put his mother behind him when he went to school. He cannot tell her, and she makes no effort to understand, his feelings and his fears. By Chapter 10, his disappointment in her misunderstanding of him forces him into greater isolation. He is repelled by her efforts to play the motherly role when she clasps him to her urgently, or speaks to him in a bright, patronising voice.

A sensitive boy   In spite of his remoteness from his mother, in Chapter 16 he is troubled because she has more to do with the Hoopers and her own affairs than with him. This shows a natural desire for affection, consistent with the sensitivity he displays throughout the novel. Kingshaw is not cold like Hooper. His emotional isolation is the result of his protective mechanism – not letting himself mind or need others. His need for affection has been suppressed because it has never been fulfilled. His mother has failed him, and his response is to force himself to manage without her. In Chapter 13 we are given a pitiful impression of his self-sufficiency through the description of how he coped with his nightmares, and his feelings of shame at having found comfort in Mr Hooper's arms.

Find examples of Kingshaw's sympathy for other people and his sentimentality towards animals.   His sensitivity and potential for affection are shown repeatedly. He is sentimental about animals, and sympathetic towards other people, even trying awkwardly to comfort Hooper when he is afraid in Hang Wood. The incident at school in which Fenwick spurns his sympathy sets a standard of bravery which Kingshaw feels he should emulate, but cannot. He envies the natural relationship between the Fieldings, recognising the contrast with the strained behaviour in his own home.

Kingshaw's compassion and concern for others – qualities which distinguish him from Hooper – are frequently shown. Compassion is at the root of his moral sense, most remarkably when he turns down the temptation to have his revenge when Hooper is at his mercy. He knows, from his own unhappy experience, that it is wrong to make others suffer, or even to wish suffering upon them. He has a superstitious fear of God's retribution, and a simple acceptance of religious teaching. This contrast between them is shown repeatedly to emphasise Kingshaw's innocence in the face of Hooper's evil behaviour.

Kingshaw's fears

Kingshaw has many fears, perhaps the result of his insecurity, and the years of coping with unhappiness. His recurrent nightmares indicate a deep unease and the suppression of his feelings.

He could contain his fears and find protection in the strategies he had developed, until he met Hooper. At Warings, all Kingshaw's problems are compounded. Every hope is stripped away, until he sees suicide as the only escape. The tragic inevitability of his suicide is convincing to the reader, because we have witnessed Kingshaw's suffering, and shared his thoughts. He is the innocent victim of Hooper's evil bullying and the adults' blind insensitivity.

MRS KINGSHAW

Character and background

Shallow
Anxious to please
Insensitive
Shows little understanding

The character of Mrs Kingshaw is deliberately undeveloped, because this novel is concerned with children and childhood. Her role is to provide a background which explains some of her son's insecurity and unhappiness. The fact that she is unaware of Hooper's treatment of Kingshaw, in spite of living closely with them, emphasises her son's isolation and suffering.

Mrs Kingshaw is a widow, struggling to manage since her husband's death. She tries to maintain her respectability by taking care of her appearance, and keeping Charles at school with the help of a charitable grant. However, she has no home of her own and no financial security. After years of moving from place to place, and living in private hotels, it is understandable that she is attracted by the possibility of a secure future with Mr Hooper at Warings.

Descriptions of Mrs Kingshaw emphasise her superficiality – the earrings and jangling bracelets, and her attention to her clothes. She is a shallow woman of limited understanding, unaware of the true impression she makes: for example, the boys at Kingshaw's school mock her, calling her 'an old tart', and Hooper sees through her flattery of his father asking Kingshaw if his mother has 'gone after' many people.

Her role as a mother

She would like to be a good mother, but is too anxious about her ability to do and say the right things. Her self-conscious efforts to relate to Charles are reflected in the artificial style of her speech, and contrast sharply with Mrs Fielding's relaxed confidence with her son.

Does Susan Hill want the reader to like and sympathise with Mrs Kingshaw?

She does not understand or feel close to Charles, but she believes that she has done her best for him. In Chapter 15 she talks about the sacrifices that she has made to keep him at school. He is embarrassed by her occasional urgent displays of affection. Every night she goes to his room to kiss him, and sometimes tries to talk to him. Unfortunately, she never really listens to what he tells her. She dismisses his feelings and his fears, simplifying them and hearing only what she wants. She seems to recognise the failings in her relationship with her son when she makes the decision to think more about herself in Chapter 5. Towards the end of the novel, she deliberately trivialises his feelings, perhaps recognising in them a threat to the future she seeks at Warings. The reader might wonder if Kingshaw has been sacrificed to the more urgent business of impressing the Hoopers. At the end of the novel, though, we see that her real fault is complete insensitivity: she looks forward to her wedding in the mistaken, but genuine, belief that it will be the best thing for both of them.

Susan Hill does not make Mrs Kingshaw's character attractive, even to Mr Hooper. Her appeal to him is in her ready praise and deferential behaviour, which give him the confidence he lacks. He fantasises about satisfying his sexual desires when they are married, but shows no affection towards her.

We are forced to recognise Mrs Kingshaw's neglect of her son's emotional needs by the emphasis on her preoccupation with her own affairs, and the false way in which she speaks to him. Her remoteness from him is emphasised by the irony (see Literary Terms) of her showering Hooper with attention when he is injured, and comforting him when they find Kingshaw dead.

She is a pitiful character, who has failed her son, and does not have the insight to recognise it, even when faced with the tragic consequences.

MR HOOPER Our interest in Mr Hooper lies in the insight he gives into the character of his son. Susan Hill writes in her introduction that, like Mrs Kingshaw, he is a deliberately two-dimensional (see Literary Terms) figure.

His physical appearance – tall, thin and dark – echoes the gloom of Warings and stirs Kingshaw's fearful memories of the crow. When Mr Hooper regards himself in the mirror, his anxiety and self-doubt are shown: he contemplates his unimpressive appearance, and tries to build up his self-confidence.

Relationships Significantly, most of the information we are given about Mr Hooper relates to his emotional inadequacy. As a child he suffered silently, not strong enough to complain, when he was made to watch his father working on his moth collection in the Red Room. The contempt that his father felt towards him contributed to his lack of confidence and drove him away. Later, his marriage to a cold and distant woman was also unhappy. The failures in his relationships with his

Weak
Complacent
Lonely
Unable to feel or
show affection

A weak man

How much is Mr
Hooper to blame
for his son's
character and
Kingshaw's
death?

father and wife, are echoed in his relationship with Edmund. He appears to have no friends, and feels resentful when Mrs Kingshaw speaks to a friend of hers on the telephone. This resentment shows that he is possessive in relationships with others – a characteristic which is shared by Edmund.

Considering his emotional inadequacy, it is not surprising that Mr Hooper is a lonely man. He cannot face being alone at Warings with its unhappy memories of childhood, or spending the summer with Edmund, whose inscrutable character makes him nervous. His isolation and inadequacy are reflected in his sexual feelings of strong desire and frustration. He is attracted to Mrs Kingshaw largely by the prospect of satisfying his desires. Her ingratiating behaviour has given him the confidence he seeks, but he has no apparent affection or regard for her.

Mr Hooper knows he has failed. He was a disappointment to his domineering and successful father, and he is aware that he is not respected by those around him. In Chapter 1 he hopes that Warings will give him the dignity and prestige that he lacks, and he tries to impress Edmund with his new status.

In spite of recognising his weaknesses, Mr Hooper is complacent. He blames other people for his problems, and feels resigned to his difficulties with Edmund, making little effort to improve things. His complacency is fuelled by deliberate ignorance of what is going on, and by the flattering support of Mrs Kingshaw. On the train journey to London with Charles in Chapter 15, the reader sees the irony (see Literary Terms) of his newly found confidence in dealing with the boys.

Whilst we might sympathise with Mr Hooper's unhappy childhood and its resulting self-doubt, we are made to acknowledge the damage done by this ineffectual man. He shirks his responsibility to guide and control his son, and is blind to Kingshaw's suffering in his care. Mr Hooper must therefore share the blame for Kingshaw's tragic death, though it is doubtful whether he has the capacity to understand or admit his part in it.

FIELDING

Character

Anthony Fielding appears in only three chapters of the novel, but he makes a strong impression on the reader, and on Kingshaw.

Confident
Well-balanced
Happy
Independent

Our first impression is of his confidence when he challenges Kingshaw about being on the altar of the church. He makes friends readily, with the easy assurance that people will accept him. His family background is secure and natural, shown briefly in his conversation at home with his mother. Fielding is a well-balanced boy. He listens sympathetically to Kingshaw's account of Hooper's bullying, unable to understand it because a boy like him would never suffer such an experience. When he comes to tea at Warings, he is sensitive to Kingshaw's feelings. He tries to protect him, but is unable to overcome Hooper's influence. On the other hand he is not excessively sentimental: he tells Kingshaw in a matter-of-fact way about the fate of the animals on his farm, and soon forgets Kingshaw's problems when he looks for slow-worms after leaving Warings with Hooper.

His role in the novel

Fielding provides a striking contrast with Kingshaw and Hooper, increasing our awareness of their problems. He also provides reassurance for the reader that childhood is not always an unhappy ordeal. Fielding represents the normal world beyond Warings, where families can be loving and secure. This world is distanced from the events at Warings to emphasise the isolation of the main characters and the obliviousness of the world to their suffering.

To Kingshaw, Fielding is a lifeline. Through this friendship, independent of Warings, he gains confidence and hope. But inevitably the relationship does not bring him happiness. Closely observing Fielding's personality and behaviour, Kingshaw feels his own inadequacies. When his mother interferes and spoils the friendship by bringing Fielding to Warings, Kingshaw's isolation is complete: there is no-one left in whom he can have confidence. Fielding illustrates the disturbing fact that simple goodwill and friendship are no match for Hooper's evil power.

LANGUAGE & STYLE

Susan Hill's style is characterised by its simplicity and sharp focus. From the opening sentence of the novel, which summarises the Hoopers' circumstances, the reader's attention is engaged and directed to important events, without detailed introduction. This economical style is well-suited to the episodic (see Literary Terms) structure of the novel. Short, clear sentences help the reader to understand the transitions in the narrative as it records the various actions and thoughts of the characters, and to follow the passage of time in the story.

LANGUAGE   Susan Hill conveys vivid images (see Literary Terms) of the characters, events and places she describes through her use of direct and easily understood descriptive language.

- She conveys images through precise description: plants and animals are named and visual details are recorded – especially in Hang Wood – reflecting Susan Hill's knowledge and love of the countryside.
- She chooses expressive verbs – a rabbit 'bumped' along harmlessly in the wood, Kingshaw begins to 'prance' on the castle walls.

- Similes (see Literary Terms) are simple and effective, sometimes reflecting children's perceptions: the tractor in Chapter 5 is like a 'great beast'; Fielding's eyelashes are like 'spiders' legs'; Kingshaw's sense of horror at the circus is conveyed by the comparison of the clown to the crow which attacked him.
- The descriptions are strongly visual, but they also appeal to other senses. In Chapter 5 the cobweb strands feel sticky and the tractor's steering wheel is damp and slippery.
- Important images recur throughout the novel – moths, the crow, Mrs Kingshaw's jewellery – reinforcing the associations of these images with characters and themes.

Language in dialogue

The dialogue between the characters is realistic, with different styles of speech giving a clear impression of the boys and their parents. Look for these features:

- The boys' speech is simple and usually short.
- Hooper and Kingshaw use slang and colloquial (see Literary Terms) expressions.
- The boys' rivalry, and need to impress each other, is reflected in aspects of their speech. They call each other 'stupid' and 'thick', and their speeches end with 'so' and 'then' to express challenge or defiance.
- Fielding's speech is different, less guarded and aggressive, to reflect his greater confidence in relating to other boys.
- The adults' speech is less natural than the boys'. They speak formally to each other, and do not express their thoughts directly.
- Mrs Kingshaw's speech is artificial and affected. The simple platitudes in her speech reflect her limited capacity to think and understand.

PART FOUR

STUDY SKILLS

HOW TO USE QUOTATIONS

One of the secrets of success in writing essays is the way you use quotations. There are five basic principles:

- Put inverted commas at the beginning and end of the quotation
- Write the quotation exactly as it appears in the original
- Do not use a quotation that repeats what you have just written
- Use the quotation so that it fits into your sentence
- Keep the quotation as short as possible

Quotations should be used to develop the line of thought in your essays.

Your comment should not duplicate what is in your quotation. For example:

> When he listens to his mother talking about the Hoopers, Kingshaw hates the voice that she uses, 'He hated the voice she put on for talking about the Hoopers'.

Far more effective is to write:

> Listening to his mother talking about the Hoopers, Kingshaw 'hated the voice she put on'.

The most sophisticated way of using the writer's words is to embed them into your sentence:

> Mrs Kingshaw's opinion that Warings is 'so satisfactory, so safe' is an ironic example of her limited understanding, and self-deception.

When you use quotations in this way, you are demonstating the ability to use text as evidence to support your ideas – not simply including words from the original to prove you have read it.

Everyone writes differently. Work through the suggestions given here and adapt the advice to suit your own style and interests. This will improve your essay-writing skills and allow your personal voice to emerge.

The following points indicate in ascending order the skills of essay writing:

- Picking out one or two facts about the story and adding the odd detail
- Writing about the text by retelling the story
- Retelling the story and adding a quotation here and there
- Organising an answer which explains what is happening in the text and giving quotations to support what you write

....

- Writing in such a way as to show that you have thought about the intentions of the writer of the text and that you understand the techniques used
- Writing at some length, giving your viewpoint on the text and commenting by picking out details to support your views
- Looking at the text as a work of art, demonstrating clear critical judgement and explaining to the reader of your essay how the enjoyment of the text is assisted by literary devices, linguistic effects and psychological insights; showing how the text relates to the time when it was written

The dotted line above represents the division between lower and higher level grades. Higher-level performance begins when you start to consider your response as a reader of the text. The highest level is reached when you offer an enthusiastic personal response and show how this piece of literature is a product of its time.

*Coursework
essay*

Set aside an hour or so at the start of your work to plan
what you have to do.

- List all the points you feel are needed to cover the
  task. Collect page references of information and
  quotations that will support what you have to say. A
  helpful tool is the highlighter pen: this saves
  painstaking copying and enables you to target
  precisely what you want to use.
- Focus on what you consider to be the main points of
  the essay. Try to sum up your argument in a single
  sentence, which could be the closing sentence of your
  essay. Depending on the essay title, it could be a
  statement about a character: Fielding's role is to
  represent normality as the happy product of a loving
  family, providing a strong contrast with Hooper and
  Kingshaw; an opinion about setting: I believe that the
  description of Warings provides an appropriate
  background for the disturbing events of this story; or
  a judgement on a theme: In her exploration of the
  characters of Hooper and Kingshaw, I believe Susan
  Hill has created a disturbing and accurate impression
  of the loneliness of childhood.
- Make a short essay plan. Use the first paragraph to
  introduce the argument you wish to make. In the
  following paragraphs develop this argument with
  details, examples and other possible points of view.
  Sum up your argument in the last paragraph. Check
  you have answered the question.
- Write the essay, remembering all the time the central
  point you are making.
- On completion, go back over what you have written
  to eliminate careless errors and improve expression.
  Read it aloud to yourself, or, if you are feeling more
  confident, to a relative or friend.

If you can, try to type your essay, using a word processor. This will allow you to correct and improve your writing without spoiling its appearance.

Examination essay

The essay written in an examination often carries more marks than the coursework essay even though it is written under considerable time pressure.

In the revision period build up notes on various aspects of the text you are using. Fortunately, in acquiring this set of York Notes on *I'm the King of the Castle*, you have made a prudent beginning! York Notes are set out to give you vital information and help you to construct your personal overview of the text.

Make notes with appropriate quotations about the key issues of the set text. Go into the examination knowing your text and having a clear set of opinions about it.

In most English Literature examinations, you can take in copies of your set books. This is an enormous advantage although it may lull you into a false sense of security. Beware! There is simply not enough time in an examination to read the book from scratch.

In the examination

- Read the question paper carefully and remind yourself what you have to do.
- Look at the questions on your set texts to select the one that most interests you and mentally work out the points you wish to stress.
- Remind yourself of the time available and how you are going to use it.
- Briefly map out a short plan in note form that will keep your writing on track and illustrate the key argument you want to make.
- Then set about writing it.
- When you have finished, check through to eliminate errors.

To summarise,
these are the
keys to success

- Know the text
- Have a clear understanding of and opinions on the storyline, characters, setting, themes and writer's concerns
- Select the right material
- Plan and write a clear response, continually bearing the question in mind

SAMPLE ESSAY PLAN

A typical essay question on *I'm the King of the Castle* is followed by a sample essay plan in note form. This does not present the only answer to the question, merely one answer. Do not be afraid to include your own ideas, and leave out some of those in the sample! Remember that quotations are essential to prove and illustrate the points you make.

How does Susan Hill arouse the reader's sympathy for Kingshaw?

Part 1:
Introduction

It is important that we feel sympathetic towards Kingshaw, so that we will believe in the likelihood of his suicide. Susan Hill arouses the reader's sympathy in several ways.

Part 2:
Narrative
technique

- Although the novel is not written in the first person, Kingshaw's thoughts are described more than anyone else's.
- Episodes are sharply focused on Kingshaw's experience, with few other details, and the description of his experience is vivid.
- The sections which deal with other characters often have unhappy implications for Kingshaw.

Part 3:
Character and
background

- He is shown as sensitive and fearful, even at the beginning.
- We understand his anxieties because we are told about his insecure family life, living in private hotels and other people's houses.

- Mrs Kingshaw's character is described in enough detail to show that she is an inadequate mother, who does not understand her son.
- The accounts of his experience at school show his vulnerability, but also an independent determination to cope, which we have to respect.
- Unlike Hooper, he is fundamentally good and kind.

Part 4:
The
relationship
with Hooper

- The descriptions of Hooper and his behaviour emphasise his cruelty and inscrutability, so we understand why Kingshaw cannot find a way to deal with him.
- Hooper dominates Kingshaw in many ways – ordering him about at Warings, and taking the lead in Hang Wood.
- Hooper appears to have ways of knowing everything, a disturbing quality which gives him power in the relationship.
- Hooper's bullying is motiveless and extreme, with Kingshaw as the innocent victim who has done nothing to provoke such malice.
- Descriptions of the worst episodes of bullying show their physical and mental effects on Kingshaw, so we see how Hooper gradually destroys him.

Part 5:
The role of
other
characters

- The adults make his problems worse by their blind insensitivity, and their plans for the future. Their weakness is despicable and arouses our sympathy for the child in their care.
- Fielding offers a brief escape, but this friendship is cruelly destroyed. Nobody can help Kingshaw.

Part 6
Suicide – the
only answer

- Kingshaw had hopes but we saw them systematically destroyed: improvement in the relationship after Hang Wood; return to St Vincent's; Hooper's 'death' following the fall; friendship with Fielding.
- By the end of the book he is isolated from every other character, especially his mother.

- The note under his door is a terrifying, and believable, promise of more persecution at school and at home.
- The stream was the only place where Kingshaw felt happy. Frequent references to it have confirmed it as a place of refuge, and prepared us for his return there at the end of the novel.

Part 7:
Conclusion

Susan Hill's skilful presentation of Kingshaw's story arouses our sympathy for him, and gives a disturbing insight into the potentially tragic consequences of a child's experience of cruelty and isolation.

FURTHER QUESTIONS

Make a plan as shown above and attempt these questions.

1 Susan Hill described the adults as two-dimensional (see Literary Terms) characters'. Do you think they have an important role in the novel?

2 Can Hooper be seen as anything other than evil? Support your answer with references to his character, background and behaviour.

3 Susan Hill has written 'settings are always very, very important to me, every bit as much as characters or themes'. What does the setting contribute to this novel?

4 Show how Susan Hill creates a vivid impression of events or places in the novel.

5 How does the novel explore the theme of isolation?

6 Describe Fielding's character and his role in the novel.

7 How realistic is Susan Hill's portrayal of childhood in *I'm the King of the Castle*?

8 Explain how the dream and flashback sections of the novel contribute to our understanding of Kingshaw's character and feelings.

PART FIVE

CULTURAL CONNECTIONS

BROADER PERSPECTIVES

Susan Hill has written about childhood in other novels and stories: the lack of understanding between mother and child was explored in *A Change for the Better* (Penguin, 1980), before she wrote *I'm the King of the Castle*, and children's fears and experience are explored in several of her short stories.

For other views of children in literature from the nineteenth century, read *Great Expectations* (Penguin Classics, 1986) or *David Copperfield* (Penguin Classics, 1985) by Charles Dickens. In both these novels, Dickens explored the lifelong significance of childhood experience to his main characters. A twentieth century novel which challenges the myth of the purity and innocence of children is William Golding's *Lord of the Flies* (Faber, 1954), in which a group of schoolboys turn to savagery when they are marooned on an island.

If you liked Susan Hill's evocation of the setting of this novel, you might enjoy her chilling ghost story *The Woman in Black* (Longman, 1989), about the haunting of a house which stands in isolation on dangerous salt marshes, exerting a terrifying influence on all who go there.

You might link your study of *I'm the King of the Castle* with media presentation of children and childhood. The innocence of children is frequently emphasised in media reports, but what happens when the child is not a victim, but an offender? Consider how newspapers deal with the issue of children's responsibility for their actions – especially when they are involved in serious crimes. Consider also the place of children in the legal process, and recent debate about appropriate sentencing of very young offenders.

colloquial a style of writing or speech which contains the kind of language and grammar associated with everyday speech

episodic a narrative which is written in the simple form of a series of episodes or incidents, rather than a complicated and involved plot

image/imagery in its narrowest sense an 'image' is a word picture, a description of some visible scene or object. More commonly 'imagery' refers to the figurative language in a piece of literature, or all the words which refer to objects and qualities which appeal to the sense and the feelings

irony a manner of speaking or writing which consists of saying one thing while you mean another. It is a method of achieving meaning via understatement, concealment and allusion, rather than by direct statement

paradox an apparently self-contradictory statement, or one that seems in conflict with all logic and opinion; yet lying behind the superficial absurdity is a meaning or truth

simile a figure of speech in which one thing is said to be like another. Similes always contain the words 'like' or 'as'

structure the overall principle of organisation in a work of literature

symbol a symbol is something which represents something else (often an idea or quality) by analogy or association

two-dimensional a figurative way of describing characters whose personalities and behaviour are not fully developed or explored by the author

TEST ANSWERS

TEST YOURSELF (Chapters 1–4)

A 1 Mrs Kingshaw *(Chapter 4)*
2 Edmund Hooper *(Chapter 1)*
3 Charles Kingshaw *(Chapter 4)*
4 Mr Hooper *(Chapter 1)*
5 The Red Room *(Chapter 1)*
6 The copse *(Chapter 3)*
7 Kingshaw's secret room *(Chapter 4)*

TEST YOURSELF (Chapters 5–9)

A 1 The dandelions *(Chapter 5)*
2 The hawthorn hedge *(Chapter 5)*
3 The sun in the clearing after the storm *(Chapter 7)*
4 The dead rabbit *(Chapter 7)*
5 Being in the stream *(Chapter 7)*
6 Kingshaw *(Chapter 9)*
7 Kingshaw *(Chapter 8)*
8 Hooper *(Chapter 8)*

TEST YOURSELF (Chapters 10–13)

A 1 Mrs Kingshaw *(Chapter 11)*
2 Mr Hooper and Mrs Kingshaw *(Chapter 10)*
3 Lesage *(Chapter 13)*
4 Mr Hooper carrying Kingshaw back to bed *(Chapter 13)*
5 Kingshaw *(Chapter 12)*

TEST YOURSELF (Chapters 14–17)

A 1 Fenwick *(Chapter 14)*
2 Fielding *(Chapter 14)*
3 Mrs Fielding *(Chapter 14)*
4 Mr Hooper *(Chapter 16)*
5 Kingshaw *(Chapter 16)*

GCSE and equivalent levels (£3.50 each)

Harold Brighouse
Hobson's Choice

Charles Dickens
Great Expectations

Charles Dickens
Hard Times

George Eliot
Silas Marner

William Golding
Lord of the Flies

Thomas Hardy
The Mayor of Casterbridge

Susan Hill
I'm the King of the Castle

Barry Hines
A Kestrel for a Knave

Harper Lee
To Kill a Mockingbird

Arthur Miller
A View from the Bridge

Arthur Miller
The Crucible

George Orwell
Animal Farm

J.B. Priestley
An Inspector Calls

J.D. Salinger
The Catcher in the Rye

William Shakespeare
Macbeth

William Shakespeare
The Merchant of Venice

William Shakespeare
Romeo and Juliet

William Shakespeare
Twelfth Night

George Bernard Shaw
Pygmalion

John Steinbeck
Of Mice and Men

Mildred D. Taylor
Roll of Thunder, Hear My Cry

James Watson
Talking in Whispers

A Choice of Poets

Nineteenth Century Short Stories

Poetry of the First World War

Advanced level (£3.99 each)

Margaret Atwood
The Handmaid's Tale

Jane Austen
Emma

Jane Austen
Pride and Prejudice

William Blake
Poems/Songs of Innocence and Songs of Experience

Charlotte Brontë
Jane Eyre

Emily Brontë
Wuthering Heights

Geoffrey Chaucer
Wife of Bath's Prologue and Tale

Joseph Conrad
Heart of Darkness

Charles Dickens
Great Expectations

F. Scott Fitzgerald
The Great Gatsby

Thomas Hardy
Tess of the D'Urbervilles

Seamus Heaney
Selected Poems

James Joyce
Dubliners

Arthur Miller
Death of a Salesman

William Shakespeare
Antony and Cleopatra

William Shakespeare
Hamlet

William Shakespeare
King Lear

William Shakespeare
The Merchant of Venice

William Shakespeare
Much Ado About Nothing

William Shakespeare
Othello

William Shakespeare
Romeo and Juliet

William Shakespeare
The Tempest

Mary Shelley
Frankenstein

Alice Walker
The Color Purple

John Webster
The Duchess of Malfi

Tennessee Williams
A Streetcar Named Desire